The local search series

Editor : Mrs Molly Harrison MBE

Graves and Graveyards

'Altar' or 'chest' tombs, Birstall, Yorkshire.

Graves and Graveyards

Kenneth Lindley ARE ATD MSIA

Photographs and rubbings by the author

London   Routledge & Kegan Paul

First published 1972
by Routledge & Kegan Paul Ltd
Broadway House, 68–74 Carter Lane,
London EC4V 5EL
Photoset and printed in Great Britain by
BAS Printers Limited, Wallop, Hampshire
© Kenneth Lindley 1972
No part of this book may be reproduced in
any form without permission from the
publisher, except for the quotation of brief
passages in criticism
ISBN 0 7100 7234 1 (C)
ISBN 0 7100 7235 X (L)

The local search series

Editor : Mrs Molly Harrison MBE

Many boys and girls enjoy doing research about special topics
and adding drawings, photographs, tape-recordings and other
kinds of evidence to the notes they make. We all learn best when
we are doing things ourselves.

The books in this series are planned to help in this kind of
'project' work. They give basic information but also encourage
the reader to find out other things ; they answer some questions
but ask many more ; they suggest interesting things to do,
interesting places to visit, and other books that can help readers
to enjoy their finding out and to look more clearly at the world
around them.

M.H.

'. . . all the business of life is to endeavour to find out what you don't know by what you do'

John Whiting *Marching Song*

Contents

Editor's preface

You may think it strange to have a book about graveyards, but until recently almost everybody was buried when they died and a monument of some kind put up in their memory, so every grave-yard is full of interesting facts about people. Some of the monuments are beautiful, some are quaint and amusing, nearly all of them have something to tell us about times very different from our own. If you look carefully, you will find as much history in graveyards as in many books; there are architecture, sculpture and engraving to be explored there too, and many wild flowers and wild creatures to watch, living happily in those quiet surroundings.

If you are planning to do a project on graveyards you will have to use your eyes and your imagination. You will need to talk to local people about your local graveyard and how it has changed, about who looks after it, who pays for it and whether there are any plans for the future. And when you are on holiday you will find it interesting to visit other graveyards and compare them with your own.

You will, of course, want to arrange the information and ideas and pictures you collect, in the best order. The chapters and headings in this book will serve as one guide, and your own ideas about arrangement are important too. Don't forget to make your work look as clear and pleasant as you can; think over whether a loose-leaf arrangement might be best, because you can then add extra sections when you like, without altering the parts that are finished. Of course you will want to include as many illustrations as possible; make sure they are well mounted, clearly labelled and arranged in the right order. Drawings, photographs, rubbings, maps and charts often tell a story better than words do, and this is as true of the story of a graveyard as of anything else.

M.H.

What to look for

Monuments of different periods

Various uses of churchyards in the past

Church monuments and non-conformist monuments

Monuments in municipal cemeteries

Death is a subject which has fascinated and mystified men for as long as we know anything about life on the earth. Very few people like to talk about it and yet some of the finest, largest and most ancient works of man are to do with it. The pyramids of Egypt are not only among the most ancient buildings, they are also among the largest and yet their only purpose was to contain bodies, and the things which the ancient Egyptians believed would be needed by the soul after death. In this country you can still see hundreds of ancient burial mounds, known as 'tumuli', built with very few primitive tools and immense effort to contain the bodies of tribal chieftains and other important people.

As civilization progressed, so monuments became more common. Our cathedrals and medieval churches are full of monuments to great churchmen, kings, soldiers, scholars and others who were important in their own times. It was not until a couple of centuries or so ago that monuments were put up to commemorate more ordinary people. By the beginning of the seventeenth century monuments to farmers, country squires, landowners, prosperous merchants or craftsmen, began to appear in the churchyards which surround our ancient churches. Within quite a short time these graveyards were filled with fascinating collections of tombstones and monuments which were added to over the years. They now make a wonderful collection from which you can learn a great deal about what people thought, what they did, how they lived and even what they looked like in times past. Old graveyards can be beautiful and interesting places, and Sir John Betjeman describes them in his poem 'Churchyards'. This is part of it :

> For churchyards then, though hallowed ground
> Were not so grim as now they sound,
> And horns of ale were handed round
> For which churchwardens used to pay
> On each especial vestry day.
> 'Twas thus the village drunk its beer
> With its relations buried near,
> And that is why we often see'
> Inns where the alehouse used to be
> Close to the church when prayers were said
> And Masses for the village dead . . .
>
> But this I know, you're sure to find
> Some headstones of the Georgian kind
> In each old churchyard near and far,
> Just go and see how fine they are.
> Notice the lettering of that age
> Spaced like a noble title-page,
> The parish names cut deep and strong
> To hold the shades of evening long,
> The quaint and sometimes touching rhymes
> By parish poets of the times,
> Bellows, or reaping hook or spade
> To show, perhaps, the dead man's trade,
> And cherubs in the corner spaces
> With wings and English ploughboy faces . . .

Burial grounds of various kinds are so much a part of the scene that few of us ever take notice of them. Churches, particularly those outside the large towns, are usually surrounded by rows of tombstones among which there may be a few trees and perhaps some larger monuments. Without such a graveyard a church somehow seems incomplete and yet few were there when the churches were first built. Apart from some Saxon gravestones the earliest tombstone known in a British graveyard is one dating from the fourteenth century which can be seen at Loversall near Doncaster.

The reason why tombstones were not common much before the

This is probably the oldest churchyard monument in England, dating from the fourteenth century, and the mason seems to have copied his design from church windows, Loversall, Yorkshire.

sixteenth century is quite simple. Before that time if you had enough money to be able to afford a monument you would have been buried inside the church. Poorer people were buried outside without a memorial, and for a century or so after tombstones became common the rich were still buried inside and those with less money outside. A man living at Kingsbridge, Devon, in the eighteenth century must have felt very strongly about this for he composed his own epitaph which reads:

Here lie I at the Chancel door
Here lie I because I'm poor
The forther in the more you'll pay
Here lie I as warm as they.

In the middle ages when churchyards had no tombstones they were often used as meeting places and they must have been the centre of village life on many occasions. The earliest structure in the churchyard was a cross, and some of these are older than the church itself. The very old ones have mostly disappeared and the bits which remain are kept inside the church, but many churchyards still have the remains of medieval crosses. These were more than just stones in the shape of a cross. In fact they were usually not cross-shaped at all. At the top of a tall shaft there would be a carving of the crucifixion beneath a stone canopy. The back was often used for some other subject. The cross shaft was mounted on a stone platform at the top of two or three steps, and these steps together with the bottom of the shaft are what you are most likely to find today.

Wandering preachers would use the cross as a platform to address the crowd and the churchyard cross was the natural place for any speaker to go to collect an audience. Many activities, including fairs, took place in the churchyard, and the first tombstones must have been regarded as a nuisance on such occasions. A painting by the artist William Hogarth shows boys playing dice on the flat top of a churchyard monument when they should have been attending church.

Different kinds of monuments

The earliest tombstones were quite simple; just a stone at the head of the grave and a smaller one at the foot. They were usually not more than 2 or 3 feet high but as tombstones became more common they began to get bigger. They also began to vary much more in shape. Many of the more expensive ones were copied from the monuments inside the church. These were rather like large boxes with a slab on the top. Inscriptions and decoration could be carved both on the top and also on each of the four sides, so these tombs could be used as family memorials over quite a long period. They are known as 'altar tombs', or 'chest tombs'. Similar ones, with the sides open, are called 'table tombs'. A large stone slab, either on top of a table or altar tomb, or horizontally on the ground is called a 'ledger'. Ledger slabs became popular at the time when bodies were dug up and stolen for medical research although they were used much earlier. It was too much trouble to shift a heavy stone and the thieves looked elsewhere. If there are any ledgers in your local churchyard see when they were most common by making a note of the dates.

During the eighteenth century, when 'classical' Greek and Roman art was fashionable, tombs were built in imitation of ancient examples. The most common of these was in the shape of an urn, usually on top of a stone pedestal. Some urns were carved with a draped cloth over them as a symbol of mourning. You can make a large collection of drawings of urns of all shapes and sizes by visiting graveyards. You can also make a list of as many different shapes of monument as you can find. Even the head-stones changed with changing fashions. By cutting silhouettes from black paper and mounting them with the dates in order you will see how simple stones were popular at one period whilst more ornate ones were common at another. The same applies to the shapes of larger monuments.

Nonconformists

So much time and money were spent on monuments in some churchyards that they were regarded by some people as a sign of arrogance or pride. The Quakers in the seventeenth and eighteenth centuries were very scathing about churchyard monuments. They called churchyards 'steeple-house yards' and dead Quakers were buried in unmarked graves around their meeting houses, or even in plots at the corners of fields. All over the country there are Quaker burial grounds, most of them still unmarked and only traceable from old documents. Later Quakers relaxed the rules a little and allowed gravestones, all of the same size and design, giving just a name and date.

Other nonconformists were as anxious as the Quakers not to be buried in churchyards although they did allow monuments. Many old chapels, particularly Baptist and Unitarian, have their own graveyards and many of these are still in use. By reading some of the epitaphs you can begin to understand how strongly the early nonconformists felt about their religious beliefs. In Scotland a group known as 'Covenanters' refused to conform to the law over their religion and they were fiercely persecuted. Covenanters' graves in various parts of Scotland tell sad tales of harsh sentences, for they were often put to death for their beliefs. On one of these monuments at Wigtown the epitaph begins:

Let earth and stone still witnes beare
Their Lyes a virgine martyre here,
Murther'd for ouning Christ supreame,
Head of His Church and no more crime.
But not abjuring presbytry,
They her condem'd by unjust law,

NCE OF LAW HANGED BY MA
JOR WINRAM FOR THEIR ADHER
ANCE TO SCOTLANDS REFOR
MATION COVENANTS NATIO
NAL AND SOLAM LEAGWE
1685

HERE LYES MARGRAT WILLSON DOUGHTER TO GILBERT WILLSON IN GLENVERNOCH WHO WAS DROOED ANNO 1685 AGED 18

LET EARTH
THIR LYES
MURTER D
HEAD OF
BUT NOT
AND HER
TEY HER
OF HEAVE
WITHIN
SHE SU
TE AC
WAS L
NEITER
COULD

*Covenanters' graves
at Wigtown, Scotland.*

Of Heaven nor Hell they stood no aw.
Within the sea tyd to a stake
She suffered for Christ Jesus Sake.

The girl whom it commemorates was drowned for her beliefs in 1685, when she was only eighteen.

Few graveyards have stories to tell as tragic as this, but most have something of interest which can show how people lived and died, what they believed and what they stood for, over very many years. Some of the things which are common in churchyards are there because of beliefs going back to times before Christianity. The evergreen trees, particularly yews, have been associated with sacred places since the times of the Druids and the ancient Greeks. They are examples of ancient customs and beliefs, sensibly 'taken over' by the early Christians and still surviving. You can still find many evergreens in graveyards, and many have been planted within the last few years. Have you ever wondered why holly and laurel are so often used for wreaths ?

Many English churchyards have been in use for nearly a thousand years. As more and more burials have taken place over

the centuries so the ground has gradually risen. That is why the ground is so much higher inside than on the outside. It is also why so many old churches seem to have been built in a hole a few feet below ground level. The wall around the edge of the churchyard has to hold the earth in as it rises above the outside level. Many of these churchyard walls are good examples of local craftsmanship and, like the tombstones, they often show the use of local materials. The photograph of Kilpeck shows a good churchyard wall.

The churchyard wall at Kilpeck, Herefordshire. The ground on the inside is level with the top of the wall.

Cemeteries

As towns grew during the last century the problem of finding space for burials became too great for the existing churchyards and chapelyards. Ground had to be purchased specially for burials and so municipal cemeteries came into being. These are owned and maintained by the local authority. Most towns now have large cemeteries and you can tell by studying the dates on the memorials how the population has grown and changed over the years. You can also see how fashions in monuments and epitaphs have changed. At the beginning of the present century, for example, angels were popular, but not many angels have been carved as memorials during the last twenty years. Another item which was once very popular but which is now no longer used is the wreath of china flowers. These were usually white, and the more expensive ones had small birds or clasped hands as well as the flowers. The whole lot was wired together and a coloured metal label was used for a message such as 'In affectionate memory'. These wreaths were placed under glass domes and most of them have now been broken or thrown away.

Rules

All municipal cemeteries have their sets of rules which tell you what you can and cannot do in them. Some types of monument are forbidden and there may also be regulations about epitaphs. The rules which apply in churchyards may be hundreds of years old. They will not only be about the care of monuments but also about such odd things as whether the vicar can keep his horse or pigs in the churchyard. All of these rules will tell you a great deal about the people who made them and about the lives of country clergymen in times past. I do not suppose that any present-day vicar would worry about whom the churchyard grass belonged to but it may have made a lot of difference a century ago when he could have let the grazing rights to a local farmer and so increased his income. The rules which apply to the local cemetery will probably be written up on a board near the entrance. For the churchyard rules you may have to ask the vicar. Try comparing these, and also finding out about any chapelyards or Quaker burial grounds in your locality.

Materials

2

Natural stone of varied colours and textures

Making a rubbing from a tombstone

Slate tombstones

Metal and wooden monuments

Artificial stone

Local stone

Most monuments are made of stone and until about a century and a half ago masons had to use the rocks which were available in their own locality. It is likely that the rock from which the oldest gravestones were cut would have come from the same quarry which provided the stone from which the church was built. This is one of the reasons why old stones often seem to look 'just right'. They are as natural to the place as the grass and trees. Some stones are better for building than for carving, and others are better for lettering than for sculpture. There is a tremendous variety of natural stone in Britain and this is shown in the wide range of colours and textures of tombstones and in the way in which they were carved. You can learn a great deal about local geology by visiting burial grounds.

In parts of the Midlands, particularly Leicestershire the building stone is a beautiful golden colour, but it is very soft. The old churches have been worn by the weather and the original parts often have to be replaced. There is, however, another local stone which is of little use for building (apart from roofs) but which makes excellent tombstones. This is slate. It is a deep grey-blue in colour and rows of slate tombstones look particularly beautiful against the warm yellow-brown of the churches. Slate is very hard but it does not crumble or chip easily so that it is very good for lettering and for some kinds of decoration. It is rather like very hard lino and the sort of cuts which the mason can make are very much like those which you do on a lino-cut. In fact the slate-carvers called themselves engravers.

Making a rubbing

Although slate is very good for lettering it is not much good for carving. Most of the decoration is therefore engraved or in low relief. Plants such as lichens find it too smooth to grow on, and the weather has little effect on it so that stones two hundred years old look as good as new. Because of this it is ideal for taking copies by rubbing. For large rubbings you need a roll of thin, tough paper such as tracing paper, and someone to hold it in place for you. It is best to start at the top and work down, rubbing with a thick greasy crayon from side to side and finishing

Taking a rubbing. All you need is a piece of thin paper and a greasy crayon.

each strip as you go. Doing it this way you can avoid the blurred effects you get when the paper moves slightly. As you reach the bottom be careful to move any grasses away from the stone, unless you want to rub these into the design.

Often you will not want to rub a whole stone, and typing paper is very good for small areas. It is easy to hold in place so that you can take rubbings on your own. The most important thing about the material which you use to rub with is that it should be greasy. Wax crayons are the best. They are quite cheap to buy and they are made in a variety of bright colours as well as black and white. You can paint over a greasy rubbing with coloured inks or watercolour paint (powder paint will not do). The water or the ink runs off the grease and into the cracks making a two-colour design and you can try out all sorts of colour mixtures. If you use black crayon on white paper then the design will show as white on black. To get the opposite effect rub with a candle and paint over it with black ink (fountain-pen ink is much better than Indian ink).

The vicar may be interested to know what you are doing if you take rubbings in the churchyard.

Slate

There are other areas where slate is the local stone. In Devon and Cornwall and parts of the Lake District it varies in colour from dark blue to grey-green. In North Wales the quarries have eaten giant steps into the mountain sides, and the graveyards filled with row upon row of slate headstones in the quarry town of Ffestiniog seem to fit beautifully into their mountain setting. As transport improved at the beginning of the last century some of the slates found their way into unexpected places. In the cemetery at Clacton-on-Sea in Essex there is a slate memorial to a Welsh seaman who was drowned when his ship sank just off the coast there. The famous Ffestiniog Railway carried slate from the quarries to ships in the harbour at Portmadoc, and the Midlands canals carried the Leicestershire slates as far north as Derbyshire and west into Lincolnshire. The dates on the stones help to tell the story of the building of the canals, and from tiny Welsh harbours such as Portmadoc and Port Dinorwic Welsh slate was exported to all parts of the world.

Other stones

Some other stones are as good for rubbings as slate, but they do not last so well. Some of these form a very hard, smooth surface but the inside of the stone gradually rots away. Eventually the surface drops off in thin sheets and only the soft centre is left, often worn into fantastic shapes but with the lettering quite unrecognizable. The illustration shows a stone which has worn away. Much of the stone found in Yorkshire and parts of Lincolnshire is like this and so is that in the Forest of Dean. The reason for the strange way in which the stone weathers is that it absorbs moisture like a sponge. As the moisture evaporates it leaves a layer of minerals on the surface. If you evaporate salty water the same thing happens and if you live in a 'hard water' area it happens all the time in your kettle. So the surface of the stone gets harder but the inside gets softer until the two fall apart.

Hard stones are usually best for lettering, but sculptors generally prefer something a little softer. Ideal stone for carving is found in various places but particularly in the Cotswolds. There the masons could use thick blocks of stone for deep-cut carving and decoration. The qualities which make it good for sculpture also make the stone unsuitable for fine lettering. It has a very coarse texture and it tends to crumble as it gets older. To overcome this much of the lettering was done on small brass plates which were then screwed on to the monuments. The lettering on these could be as small and as finely engraved as you wished. Metal plates were used in a number of areas where the stone was not good for lettering.

Metal monuments

Sometimes metal was used for the whole monument, or for parts of it other than lettering. Small pieces of sculptured decoration cast in lead or iron were occasionally used even on small head-stones when the stone was unsuitable for carving. These are not very common and if you come across one you should make a careful note of the place, and the date of the monument. It is quite a 'find'. You should be able to make a copy of such small castings by pressing a slab of plasticine over the sculpture and so reproducing the original mould. This needs great care and

An eroded tombstone, Aberford, Yorkshire.

Lettering engraved on a brass plate, Bisley, Gloucestershire.

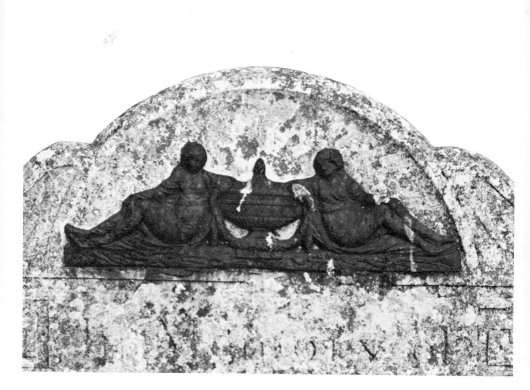

Cast iron decoration set into a stone at Long Melford, Suffolk.

patience. The plasticine can then be used as a mould for plaster, or as a base for papier mâché. In either case you can paint the result, either to match the original or in colours of your own choice. Many tombstones and monuments were originally painted all over in bright colours and you can often find bits of the original paint sticking to the surface in places.

Metal monuments, particularly those made from cast iron, were also painted. Cast iron has been used for monuments since the seventeenth century and until the invention of modern methods of casting, iron-founding was a local industry wherever iron-ore and wood for charcoal were available. We think of iron-casting in terms of enormous foundries in places like Sheffield, but it was often carried out in small workshops in rural areas. The main work of these foundries would be to produce farm implements or cooking pots, but some of them also produced memorials. The churchyard at Long Melford in Suffolk

has a number of iron 'gravestones' which were made in the village, and you can find odd ones here and there in most parts of the country. It is worth trying to find out where these were made, and the maker usually cast his name somewhere on each monument. The earliest modern foundry was at Coalbrookdale, Shropshire, where Abraham Darby first made iron by using coke instead of charcoal, at the beginning of the eighteenth century. The Coalbrookdale foundries became world famous for their products (their catalogues contained everything from massive fountains to fire-backs) and included among these was a selection of memorials.

The simplest were adaptations from gravestones, much thinner but generally the same shapes. The more elaborate ones offered a choice of columns and urns and a variety of plinths, decorative railings and so on. Where these have been kept painted to prevent rust they look as good as new and there are

Madeley, Shropshire: cast iron from nearby Coalbrookdale, painted and as good as new after a hundred years.

still plenty to be found, particularly in the area around the foundry. By the middle of the last century railings were commonly used around most larger memorials whether or not the monument itself was of iron. Earlier in the century iron grilles were sometimes placed over graves to prevent the bodies from being stolen.

Wood

Of all the natural materials available stone is obviously the best for memorials. Iron is a natural material but it is not used in its original state. The other natural substance most frequently used was wood, but this does not last as long as stone or metal and most of the older wooden memorials have long since rotted away. When wood was used it was either because it was easier to find locally than stone or because it was cheaper. In areas such as the Chilterns and parts of Suffolk and Sussex where stone was very scarce wooden monuments had to be used. The commonest shape for these was a post at each end joined by a plank. Because they look like bedsteads they were often called 'bed-boards'. The inscription had to be painted on to the plank and this was a job not for the mason but for the sign painter. It must often have been done by the wheelwright or wagon builder because painting was part of their jobs.

New materials and new ways of transport

Until the railways and canals opened up new transport routes memorials had to be made from the materials which were readily available near at hand. By the middle of the last century you could choose a tombstone or monument from a catalogue, just as you can today, and strange stones began to appear in English churchyards. One of the oddest was made artificially, rather like pottery, and called Coade Stone. Coade Stone monuments were sold all over the country and many survive. They all have the name 'Coade' on them somewhere and they are usually fairly smooth, and yellowish in colour. Nowadays large numbers of white marble stones are imported from Italy, and they look very out of place as well as weathering badly.

How many different stones can you find? Make a list of all the

Two decayed wooden grave boards at New Mill Baptist Chapel, Hertfordshire.
These were once common in some areas where stone is scarce. The
inscription would be painted along the side.

materials in your local graveyards and try to find out where they came from. The dates are important for they often indicate when a local railway or canal was first opened. Is local stone still used and if so where is it quarried? Ask your local mason what stones he uses and whether anyone ever asks him for such materials as slate or cast iron. These are by far the most durable of materials so far used for graveyard monuments.

Lettering

3

The lettering on tombstones as varied as that in books

Roman lettering; pen lettering and other kinds

When reading the inscriptions on tombstones have you ever noticed how many different kinds of lettering are used? We are so accustomed to reading all kinds of lettering that most of us hardly notice that the letters themselves can be of many different shapes and sizes and yet still be recognized. Think of a particular letter (for example E) and see how many different ways you can find of writing, printing or painting it. It comes as a surprise to most people to find that the lettering on tombstones, at least until the present century, is as varied as that to be found anywhere else. In fact some masons in the middle of the nineteenth century seem to have taken a great deal of trouble to include as many different kinds of lettering as possible on each tombstone.

Look at the photograph of part of a tombstone from Saddleworth, Yorkshire, and see how many different alphabets the mason has used. It looks as though he had bought himself a book of alphabets and tried to use as many as possible. The effect is very decorative. It is very likely that he used a catalogue from a firm making printer's type to copy his letters from but he

'Egyptian' letters, Rothley, Leicestershire.

SACRED
TO THE MEMORY OF
SARAH ANN, DAUGHTER OF
WILLIAM AND BETTY ROBINSON
OF
BENTFIELD
who departed this Life January
1852, in the 1st Year of her Age

Fine lettering at Saddleworth, Yorkshire

has cut them into the stone with great skill. If you have ever tried to 'lay out' a page of lettering you will know how difficult this is. To do it so well and then to cut the letters shows just how good this particular mason was at his job. The surprise is that masons all over the country were doing just as well, and their work is so little thought of that many of these stones are being broken up or removed.

Roman letters

The alphabet which we use is known as the Roman alphabet because it is based upon that perfected by the Romans in the second century. The illustration on p. 21 shows some lettering from the inscription of a Roman monument in Italy and you can see what a beautiful design it is and how well it has survived for

A fragment of a Roman second-century inscription.

*'Roman'-style lettering,
Foremark, Derbyshire.*

nearly two thousand years. It is difficult to believe that each of the alphabets used by the Saddleworth mason is derived from the one used in ancient Rome. Different materials and different uses have produced many different letter shapes but so long as the basic shapes are the same and the letters remain recognizable (sometimes only just) then they are all 'Roman' alphabets.

The earliest Tombstones

It was not until the sixteenth and seventeenth centuries that gravestones as we know them began to be made. The masons who carved these were country craftsmen more skilled at mending a barn than at lettering. The lettering which they used was often very simple, and sometimes included spelling mistakes. If they could not fit a word in they did not hesitate to finish it with small letters over the top of the others or to run the ending into some decoration round the edge. At that time there were no 'standard' dictionaries and the mason had to make up his own mind about the spelling. He also had to take decisions about the letters themselves, for there were several versions of some of them in common use. The S, for example, was sometimes as we know it today and sometimes like an 'f' with the cross-stroke shortened. There were also two kinds of lettering in common use. One, known as 'Gothic' (or to a printer, 'blackletter') was based on medieval books written with a quill pen. The other was what we would now call 'Roman', looking much more like the original version.

During the eighteenth century Roman art and architecture were greatly admired and it was the fashion to copy them. Fashionable people therefore expected their monuments to have inscriptions in good Roman letters. If you look in graveyards, particularly in those areas such as the Cotswolds where wealthy people liked to live, you will find many examples of monuments with eighteenth century lettering. As in earlier times some country masons were not quite up to the task of producing such fashionable lettering, but their own versions of it are often original and sometimes more interesting. Look at the rubbing from a stone at Gaddesby, Leicestershire. Although the mason has used the thick and thin strokes of the Roman alphabet he has added his own curly pieces of decoration. Notice how he has shortened 'The' in the second line.

Gaddesby, Leicestershire.

Pen letters

During both the eighteenth and nineteenth centuries the art of writing with a pen was considered to be an essential part of education. Writing masters taught the sons and daughters of the wealthy how to write correctly, and exercises were set both in lettering and in decoration. One of the most famous of these masters was John Baskerville, well known as a printer and designer of type, who also engraved tombstones. The most successful of these writing masters published copy-books which

Inscription based on pen lettering, Padstow, Cornwall.

were engraved on copper plates for printing. So it is that we call the kind of writing which they taught 'copperplate', and it was still being taught at the beginning of the present century.

Many different alphabets

If you look again at the Saddleworth tombstone (p. 20) you will see three figures, including an angel blowing a trumpet. These were probably copied from a book on copperplate lettering, for they have the swirly, flowing lines which you get when you use a pen with a flexible nib, or a sharpened quill. The word 'sacred' is in Gothic letters although this and the other lines were copied from a typefounders' catalogue. In the second line 'the memory' is in letters with curly ends to each stroke and these are called 'Tuscan'. You do not often see them today but they were very popular at the time for all kinds of decorative uses from fairgrounds to toffee labels. The third line is in letters with no thick-and-thin strokes and no decorative strokes. These are called 'sans serifs' and the mason has made them more interesting by cutting an outline round each letter. The word 'of' below this has been carved as though it was on a brass plate, like the one which would be screwed on to the coffin. Even the screw heads have been put in. It would be difficult to imagine a more decorative piece of lettering than that found on this tombstone.

Two other illustrations on pp. 26, 27 show similar headstones in different parts of the country. How many kinds of lettering can you see on these, and how many can you find in your local

Sans-serif lettering, Bridestowe, Devon.

'Tuscan' letters, Stanford-on-Soar, Leicestershire.

burial grounds? Notice how different modern gravestones are from these. If you take rubbings from old stones and look at some of the decorative alphabets used it is difficult to think of such lettering being allowed on tombstones today. If you look at modern memorials you will soon see that most of the lettering is the same and very little of it is as good as on the older stones. Why do you think this is? Perhaps you think that some of the older stones are too decorative, or not solemn enough?

If the stones in your district are suitable for rubbing you could make a book of different alphabets, mounting different examples on sheets of coloured paper and joining them together like a concertina. Sometimes you may be able to rub a whole tombstones, and such rubbings can make very exciting wall decorations. A row of them in different colours could look very good on your classroom wall and you could try copying the

Bridestowe, Devon: many designs of alphabets, beautifully engraved on local slate and perfectly preserved for more than a century (the mason's name is near the top of the right-hand stone).

THIS STONE IS

ERECTED

IN AFFECTIONATE

REMEMBRANCE OF

HENRY FROGGATT

who departed this Life

October 16; 1840,

AGED 21 YEARS

Varieties of lettering on slate at Twyford, Derbyshire.

various letters from them. Many nineteenth century masons liked to design their own variations of alphabets which they had seen. See if you could do the same. If you are able to produce a book of lettering it would be interesting to take it to a stonemason to find out whether anyone has ever asked him for such letters on a gravestone, and you might also ask your vicar whether he would allow a modern stone with such decorative lettering in his churchyard. If not, then ask the reason why.

Letters copied from printer's type, Bridestowe, Devon.

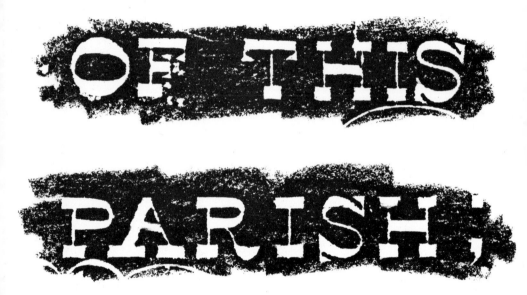

Inscriptions

4

Epitaphs: sentimental, warning, comic or praising ones

Epitaphs describing adventures and accidents

Epitaphs are verses composed for use on monuments. For centuries people have been fascinated by them. Some people write them, others collect them. Very many books have been published containing collections of epitaphs and they are still very popular. The best collections of all are those which you make for yourself, and they are very easy to make. All you need is a notebook in which to write down any interesting examples which you may find. Then you might like to copy them out in a book with your own illustrations. If you carry the notebook about with you and copy more examples down whenever you have time to look in a graveyard you will soon fill your notebook. You will find that some epitaphs occur over and over again, whilst others must have been written especially for one tombstone.

There have always been fashions in epitaphs as in most other things. Sometimes people preferred what we would probably think of as very sentimental verses, particularly about children. At other times most of the epitaphs warn the reader that he will one day die and that he had better make sure that he will be ready when the time arrives. Most of the verses must have been written, like popular songs of the time, by unknown poets, rather like the people who nowadays write the verses for greetings cards. Sometimes you may come across the work of a well-known poet or a verse of a popular hymn.

Some of the oldest inscriptions in graveyards are those which are intended to warn the readers of their own fate, and they occur all over the country on tombstones from the seventeenth to the nineteenth century. Can you imagine what sort of a person would want such a verse as this on his tombstone?

All you that come my grave to see
What I am now so you must be
Grieve not for me my glass is run
His will be done.

Different versions of this are very common, particularly from the eighteenth century, and it is interesting to try and find as many as you can. People at that time would probably know better than we do the meaning of the phrase 'my glass is run'. Do you know what it refers to?

By the end of the century warnings are still quite common but the verses are usually less direct about death. As in the carvings, flowers are used as symbols, and children are often described as 'buds' in lines such as

This lovely bud so young and fair
Called home to early doom.

In a Leicestershire churchyard the epitaph to a boy of fourteen who died in 1769 starts with a flower used as a symbol of life, and ends with the usual warning.

My rose was cropt just in the bloom
My rising sun went down at noon
In youth and strength put not your trust
The strength of living is but dust.

We would not think of putting such a verse on a grave today but you can read some which are not very different from these in the 'deaths' columns of your local newspaper. Can you find out who writes these? Often you will find various lines in epitaphs put together in different ways as if someone had written down half a dozen or so and then changed lines from one to another. Although flowers are the commonest symbols, in verses as well as in sculpture, others often occur. Symbols are rather like badges or 'trade marks'. They are pictures or objects which represent ideas. The hour-glass is often referred to, particularly in times when clocks were a rarity. A sailor's grave might have a verse such as the following :

His anchor was the Holy Word
His rudder blooming hope
The love of God his main topsail
And faith his sailing rope.

See how many different symbols you can find in epitaphs. Illustrate them with drawings of symbols found in the decoration of tombstones.

IN MEMORY OF
HANNAH TWYNNOY
Who died October 23rd 1703
Aged 33 Years.

In bloom of Life
She's snatch'd from hence.
She had not room
To make defence:
For Tyger fierce
Took Life away.
And here she lies
In a bed of Clay.
Until the Resurrection Day.

A powerful, poetic epitaph at Malmesbury, Wiltshire.

The sailor's epitaph not only tells us about his job but also shows something of his religious beliefs. You will find many epitaphs which describe death as 'God's will' and go on to mention belief in the resurrection.

Some are even more definite about religious beliefs, like this from the Baptist graveyard at Loughborough:

Tis Religion that can give
Solid pleasure while we live.
Tis religion can supply
Solid comfort when we die.
After death its joy will be
Lasting as Eternity.

Not all epitaphs are as serious as this, and it is surprising how many are amusing. Some appear to us as quite funny, although they were probably meant to be serious. I wonder what we are meant to think about this, at Church Stretton:

On a Thursday she was born
On a Thursday made a bride
On a Thursday her leg was broke
And on a Thursday died.

Old books on epitaphs are full of very funny examples but most of these have disappeared. Victorian clergymen did not like to have funny verses in their churchyards and I doubt if they would be allowed today. Perhaps it is a pity that we can no longer find verses like the following, formerly in a Norfolk churchyard:

Here lies Matthew Mud
Death did him no hurt
When alive he was Mud
And now, dead, he's but dirt.

There are a surprising number of amusing epitaphs still to be found, and you cannot help wondering whether some of the people whom they commemorate would have approved. In some cases there is no doubt, for they wrote them themselves and left instructions that the verses were to be inscribed on their tombstones.

A schoolmaster at Emley, Yorkshire, had this verse carved and

set into the churchyard wall as his memorial when he died in
1732 :

If fortune keep thee warm
Thy friends about thee swarm
Like bees about a honey pot
But if she frown & cast thee down
Lye there and Rott.

Not all inscriptions are sad, or funny. Many of them tell of kind
deeds or people who were generous. In past generations, before
the National Health Service or unemployment pay poor people
suffered a great deal when they were ill or out of work. Occasionally wealthier people were known for their kindness whilst they
were alive, or they left sums of money to help the poor when
they died. A Worcestershire woman who died in 1880 'be-
queathed one hundred and fifty pounds for the benefit of the
aged poor of this parish. The interest to be distributed by the
Vicar of Beckford for the time being in coals annually at
Christmas for ever.' It is not unusual to find such acts recorded on
tombstones and they are often a sign of the way in which a local
squire or lady would feel responsible for the villagers whom they
knew. Nowadays it is more likely that the money would be left
to a charity such as Oxfam.
Sometimes a less wealthy person would be remembered because
he was good or honest, such as the Wantage man who died in
1821 whose epitaph tells that

He toil'd through life with honest fame
And left behind a pure good name
When life is past and death is come
Then well is he that well has done.

If people were killed in an accident or by some other unusual
misfortune it was nearly always recorded on their tombstone.
In the days before radio and television a local crime would be
talked about for a very long time and a murder would arouse a
great deal of interest among folk whose daily lives were rather
dull. If the murder was particularly brutal, songs would be composed about it, or plays written about it, the most famous of
which was 'Maria Martin and the Red Barn' about a murder in
Essex. Places which had never been heard of became famous

overnight and inquisitive people flocked to the scene of the dreadful deed. A ledger stone in Saddleworth churchyard tells a typical story :

> Here lie interred and dreadfully bruised and lacerated bodies of William Bradbury and Thomas his son, both of Greenfield who were together savagely murdered in an unusually horrid manner on Monday night Ap. 2 1832.
>
> Throughout the land wherever news is read,
> Intelligence of their sad death has spread ;
> Those now who talk of far fam'd Greenfield hills,
> Will think of Bill o' Jacks and Tom o' Bills.
>
> Such interest did their tragic end excite
> That, ere they were removed from human sight,
> Thousands on thousands daily came to see
> The bloody scene of the catastrophe.

Other verses follow and so not only a remote moorland hamlet but also the nicknames of two of its inhabitants are recorded and remembered.

All sorts of odd accidents are recorded on tombstones, from that of a soldier buried in Winchester who died 'by drinking cold small beer' to a man killed at Milton Regis, Kent, in 1696 'by means of a rockett'. Guy Fawkes's night has been the cause of accidents for three hundred years. Other kinds of accidents, such as drowning or falling off a horse are frequently recorded. When large numbers of farm labourers were employed on the land it is surprising how many seem to have been killed by lightning. At Stanton Harcourt there is a monument to 'an industrious young man and virtuous maiden of this parish, contracted in marriage, who being with many others at harvest work were both in one instant killed by lightning on the last day of July 1718'. It is very doubtful if they would have been remembered today if they had not been killed in such a way. Sometimes lightning was thought of as God's judgment on a wrongdoer, and recorded as such on a monument.

Inscriptions tell us a great deal about people, both famous and unknown, and how life has changed over the centuries. If you make notes of all the interesting ones which you can find you may well be keeping the only record of some interesting but forgotten event or person. The best stones decay eventually and there are many good inscriptions which are becoming difficult or impossible to read. A rubbing is sometimes a help in trying to read a worn stone. If you have a camera it is useful to take a photograph when the light is coming from the side and so casting shadows from the slightest bump on the surface. You will often have to dig down, or remove ivy to find parts of an epitaph but it is worth while if you can find something which may have been hidden or forgotten for many years. Your books of epitaphs could easily be an important record of local history. It will almost certainly be interesting to read and even more interesting to collect, write and illustrate. Could *you* write a suitable or amusing epitaph for yourself, or for your pet or your friend ?

5

Signs and symbols

Hidden meanings in many tombstone decorations

Skulls, skeletons, hour-glasses, wings and other details

Every time you walk down a road you will see signs which give you all kinds of information. If you are driving a car you have to learn which signs tell you about one-way streets, or pedestrian crossings or school entrances and so on. Very few of these signs need lettering on them because we can learn to understand signs and symbols just as easily as we can words. A century or so ago signs were necessary as many people could not read. In India even today signs are used on voting papers at elections because many voters cannot read the candidates' names. Before education in Britain was compulsory for everybody (do you know how long ago that was?) signs were used very much more than they are today. Even now, although most people can read, signs are still very necessary.

You can easily find signs which were in use at a time before most people could read. Mile-posts often have pointing fingers on

St Mawes, Cornwall.

them to show the way to a particular town. Your local church probably has a cross on the top because people recognized this as the symbol for Christianity. Centuries ago the fish was used to symbolize Christianity. History is full of signs and symbols and there is no better place to look for them than in an old graveyard.

If you visit seaside churchyards you are often told that the gravestones with skull and crossbones on them were those of pirates, but this is nothing more than a good story. Skulls and bones were the commonest ways of showing that death comes to all of us, and our ancestors were very fond of telling each other how short life can be. One of the commonest of all epitaphs is :

Reader pause as you pass by
As you are now so once was I
As I am now so must you be
And so prepare to follow me

There are many variations of this verse, all saying much the same thing. Are there any in your local churchyard ? Write down as many as you can by visiting old graveyards, arrange them in order of date, and notice how the spelling changes.

It seems strange to us that people should want to be reminded of death, but old monuments often have several of these signs of mortality. Skeletons are quite common, but Father Time also appears perhaps with an hour-glass (to show time running out).

An hour-glass for time and bones for mortality at High Hoyland, Yorkshire.

Another way of showing the passing of time was to carve an hour-glass with two wings, one of a bird, indicating day, and the other of a bat for night. Hour-glasses were used for telling the time before cheap clocks were made, and there was usually one inside the church to remind the priest not to take too long over his sermon. Now we only use them as egg-timers.

Can you find any other designs which show the passing of time, or think of any which would be suitable for use today? Perhaps the expression 'time flies' has something to do with wings on tombstones.

*Painswick,
Gloucestershire: a
reminder of death.*

Wings also appear on monuments for a rather different reason. You will often find at the top of a stone, above the lettering, a face with wings on either side of it. This was meant to show the soul of the dead person flying up to Heaven. Some of these carvings of souls are very old. What is the earliest that you can find?

During the eighteenth century when many country gentlemen were having their houses rebuilt in the new, fashionable Italian style, the winged souls on country tombstones began to look like the chubby little cherubs in Italian painting. Sometimes this

Burton Lazars, Leicestershire.

was because the masons employed to work on the mansions also carved tombstones when they were not working on buildings. Country masons saw what was going on and tried to copy the fashionable styles in their own way. Some of the results are very amusing. They did the same with angels, some of which look like country girls dressed up for a village fête. If you cannot take rubbings of these because the stone is too rough, then the decorations make good subjects for lino-cuts, and you could make a book of these, with epitaphs written in.

Another very common symbol on funeral monuments is an urn. Why do you think this was so? Where they are engraved into slate they make very decorative rubbings, and no two ever seem to be quite the same. Sometimes they have little texts carved on the side, and often they are draped over as a sign of grief. As you would expect, grief is often shown, and in many different ways. Weeping figures are quite common, and these are not as easy to design as you might think: try and draw or model one and you will find out.

Willoughby-on-the-Wolds, Nottinghamshire.

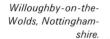

Flowers for remembrance, an urn for ashes and drapery for decoration on a Victorian gravestone at Haltwhistle, Northumberland.

DIED 10TH SEPTR 1883, AGED 6 WEEKS
"SAFE IN THE ARMS OF JESUS"

The weeping willow tree is an obvious symbol, and weeping figures are sometimes shown sitting underneath one. If you can find any weeping figures notice what costumes they are wearing. Do you think that they were meant to be portraits? The Victorians were fond of showing affection as well as grief and their memorials include hearts (rather like Victorian Valentines), clasped hands or even pairs of doves sitting on a nest.

It is very unusual to find a crucifix on an English tombstone and even crosses were rare until the end of the last century. Why was this? Perhaps your history teacher could tell you. Other religious symbols do occur quite frequently, particularly those which show a belief in life after death. One of the oldest symbols of hope is the anchor, so do not make the mistake of thinking that any tomb with an anchor on it is that of a sailor. Open books represent the Bible and the Last Judgment and a ring is one of the oldest known symbols, representing eternity. Often the ring is in the form of a snake with its tail in its mouth. On other stones the Eye of God is shown looking down from a cloud.

New Mill Baptist Chapel, Hertfordshire: a Victorian way of showing affection and a belief that the family would be reunited in Heaven.

*The eye of God,
Bridestowe, Devon.* Many of the symbols which you find in graveyards have been in use since before Christian times and for that reason some of them were forbidden within the past century. Flowers have always been popular as symbols. They were used at funerals of the Pharaohs of ancient Egypt and we still send wreaths today. What symbols would you suggest putting on a tombstone? It is interesting to make a collection of symbols from monuments, using drawings, photographs or rubbings, and to make them into a book showing the dates, the place where you found each one and, if possible, where the symbol was first used.

Family life

6

Children's tombstones and servants' tombstones

Fashions in names

We learn a great deal from books, television, films and magazines about how life has changed over the past two or three hundred years. We all know that cars have taken the place of stage-coaches and that radio has made it possible to send messages across the world as quickly as talking to the person next to you. Museums often have interesting collections of 'local bygones' which illustrate many of these changes in everyday life. What is not so obvious, although just as interesting, is the way in which family life has changed.

For one thing, families have become much smaller. In the days when your great-grandparents lived, families with between ten and twenty children were not uncommon. There are not many families as large as this today. Although most parents a century ago had large numbers of children it was very rare for all of them to survive and illnesses which many of you may have had would at one time have killed many children of your age.

Many old people now live much longer than they would have done a generation ago, for the same reason. We can all expect to live longer and to suffer less from illnesses than our ancestors. Because of this family life has changed a great deal. The girls who now leave school to find jobs would probably have stayed at home to help look after the house and their brothers, sisters and grandparents, had they lived in the last century.

If they had been born into a poor family then they would most likely have become domestic servants. All but the poorest families had at least one servant. Now, I expect that your mother has to do all her own housework, shopping and cooking. It is very unlikely that any of you will try to find work as domestic servants.

Children

The changes in family life have had a great effect on the lives of children. Those in well-off families are no longer dressed like dolls and expected to be 'seen and not heard'. Those in poorer families are not sent out to work at the age of six or seven. They are also likely to be stronger and healthier.

Some illnesses, such as diphtheria, which are now very uncommon because of immunization, were frequently fatal before the discovery of modern drugs. If you read the inscriptions in old graveyards you will find many monuments to children and quite a lot of them died from diseases which are now almost unknown or not thought of as serious. An epitaph at Brightlingsea, Essex, tells a sad but common tale :

Under these clods lyeth the Dodds
Four Children here the earth encloseth
Elizabeth John Sarah and Joseph
Likewise their mother Sarah Dodd
Whose Soul I hope doth rest with God . . .

Here lies enclosed Elias Dodd
    His wife and Children Small
I hope they rest among the Blest
    And Pray God Save us all.

On this stone we are not told what caused the deaths of the Dodd children, or their ages, but these facts are often recorded on tombstones. At More, in Shropshire, the epitaph to a child of two who died in 1767 tells us

Loe here he lies free from all care & strife
By spots he died tho' spotless was his life.

Childbirth itself was far more dangerous than it is now and there are many rather sad memorials to babies and their mothers who died together. The illustration on page 45 shows a mother and her baby. Do you think that the carving was intended as a portrait ? Notice whether the clothes shown are those which were fashionable a hundred and fifty years ago. Carvings of mothers and children are not as common as epitaphs. One in a

Cwmyoy, Monmouth-shire: mother and child. Many more children died very young before modern drugs and vaccination prevented otherwise fatal illnesses.

churchyard on Portland shows a mother in bed with two babies, and an angel hovering above.

A slate headstone at Burton Lazars in Leicestershire has a carving of a mother feeding her baby, with two other children. Are there any carvings of mothers and their children in your area?

Illness

Although there are still many illnesses which cannot be cured we are far better off in this respect than at any other period in history. We think of plagues as something from the middle ages, but outbreaks of such diseases as cholera caused large numbers of deaths until well into the last century. When this happened it was common to bury the victims all together in an unused part of the churchyard. You can sometimes find a notice on the church wall describing the outbreak and telling you how many people died and where they were buried. Many people suffered a great deal. Nowadays we would be able to cure many of the diseases from which people suffered, or to ease their pain. In the last century those who suffered could only look forward to death to relieve their pains. One of the commonest of epitaphs, found in graveyards all over England is this :

Affliction sore long time I bore
Physicians were in vain
Till God did please my soul to ease
And set me free from pain.

There are many slight variations of this verse and you could fill a book with them. Another very common nineteenth-century epitaph concerns a disease which has been almost wiped out within quite recent times :

The pale consumption gave the final blow
The stroke was fatal but the effect was slow
With wasting pain I sorely was oppressed
Till God was pleased by death to give me rest.

Servants
Life in previous centuries must have been very hard for many people and it was not only invalids who longed for rest. Many hard-working housewives did the same. A servant's life must have been one of almost unbearable drudgery at times. There are still one or two tombstones surviving which record the deaths of Negro slaves. Sometimes these slaves were brought to England and treated well by kindly masters, and it was very fashionable to have a Negro servant in the eighteenth century. A Negro who was born a slave is buried at Old Kirkbraddan on the Isle of Man and his tombstone records that it was put there

by 'a grateful master in memory of a faithful servant'. The epitaph to another Negro, buried in a Bristol churchyard, begins:

I who was born a Pagan and a Slave
Now sweetly sleep a Christian in my grave
What tho' my hue was dark my Saviour's sight
Shall change this darkness into radiant light.

It was common for masters to pay for monuments to their servants. Although the hours worked by servants were long and their pay very small many of them seem to have been quite happy and many country men and women went into domestic service in preference to farm labouring or other jobs. Sometimes they stayed with the same family for their whole lives, starting when they were children and staying until they were too old to work any more.

In the large country houses there would be very many servants doing different kinds of work. They included cooks, butlers, parlour maids, coachmen, ostlers, grooms, gardeners and many others. A butler or head gardener would be proud of his position, which was one of importance and responsibility, and it would probably be mentioned on his gravestone. On a big estate there would be work connected with both the house and the grounds and farms belonging to the family. At West Rasen in Lincolnshire a tombstone illustrates how much the people in a country district sometimes relied on a landowner or large estate for their living.

'To the memory of George Searby, cottager, for many years largely entrusted with the disposal of the produce of land, who died June 20 1857 aged 71 years. This stone is erected by contributions from his employers in acknowledgement of his care and fidelity.'

It is not an epitaph which you can imagine being written today. A good employer looked after his servants and employees but he regarded them almost as his own property and it would have been almost impossible for a servant to change his or her job without the consent of their employer. There are even gravestones which record how a servant changed from one master to another when the first died. One in a Rutland churchyard tells the story of one servant who started work when he was ten and then changed from one family to another (having been recommended for his services) and died in service when he was eighty.

Memorials to servants were at one time so common that in 1891 a book was published which contained nothing but epitaphs to servants. If you search carefully you will still find enough to make a list of the various jobs which they did, the length of time which they spent in service, and the things which their masters said about them. From these you can begin to get a good idea of the place of servants in families, both rich and less well off, in the last century.

Names

You may think it strange that servants were so common until quite recent times. Another change which appears strange is the fashion for different names. If you make a list of the names of your friends you can easily discover which were the most common at the time when you were born. Nowadays it is quite common for a television series or popular actor to make a Christian name popular. In the last century it could be a popular hero or (more likely) a character from the Bible. One of the most interesting things you can do in old graveyards is to collect names. Always record the date, and see if you can discover which names were the most popular at any particular time. Some names, such as John, have remained popular for centuries, but is anyone ever named Algernon, Marmaduke, Nellie or Jemima nowadays? These were not uncommon a hundred years ago. Why do you think names have changed so much? Can you find any Victorian names which you really like? Some of them are becoming quite fashionable again.

By reading epitaphs you will discover how family life has changed, and how in other ways it has remained the same. Some families seem to have lived happily together whilst others had quarrels which even death could not mend. There are monuments to much-loved parents from their children and verses to children from bereaved parents. It is surprising how many people took the trouble to write epitaphs to young children when you think how common it was for children to die young. It is obvious

that the loss felt by parents was no less because of this. Sometimes it must almost have seemed that children were doomed to
die young. A gravestone to a man at Sapperton has this inscription :

> A bitter cup, a shock severe
> To part with one we lov'd so dear
> Our loss is great, we'll not complain
> But trust in Christ to meet again.

> Also four children of the above, Thomas (aged 9 months),
> Mary Eliza (6 months), Julia Augusta (11 years), George (9
> years).

The date was 1878. Perhaps we are fortunate to be living a
hundred years later ?

7   Trade and industry

Many different occupations described on tombstones

Country trades and newer industries

Gravestones connected with canals, railways, ships and aircraft

You will know the old rhyme about 'the butcher, the baker, the candlestick maker' but have you ever thought about what happened to candlestick makers? When the verse was first written they must have been quite common, but like many other trades and professions they have disappeared. As new inventions replace old skills and new ideas change our way of life, so occupations change to meet new needs. Men were often proud of their trade or profession and wanted to be remembered for what they did, and it was quite common, particularly in the last century, for occupations to be recorded on gravestones.

In an old graveyard you can sometimes build up a fascinating picture of life in the past by making a list of jobs which people did then, and trying to find out about occupations which no longer exist. At Henbury, near Bristol, there is the grave of a 'running footman' and if you can discover what sort of job he did it will give you a good idea of how an eighteenth-century gentleman might have regarded his servants.

Shepherd's crook and shears, Burton Lazars, Leicestershire.

In Memory of
David Roberts Merch.ᵗ
and Harp-Maker.
who died at Liverpool
June 23ᵈ 1779. Aged 48 Years

Many occupations are what you might expect, even today. Burial grounds near the coast have their share of captains, officers of excise, lighthouse-keepers or ship's chandlers (the word 'chandler' comes from the French for candle and so indicates what sort of stores were once important on board ship). A small, prosperous inland town would have a different list. In a graveyard at Loughborough you can find a cabinet-maker, apothecary, butcher, cutler, carrier, grocer, plumber, schoolmaster, draper, inn-keeper, architect, auctioneer, carpenter, hatter, farmer, supervisor of excise, clerk to the magistrates and toolmaker. How many of these do you think you might find in the town now? Sometimes the decoration on a stone shows something of the occupation of the person commemorated, and we can learn a great deal from such carvings. Can you see the scissors at the

Llanrwst, Denbighshire: a very unusual occupation. Even in 1779 it was obviously not a full-time job.

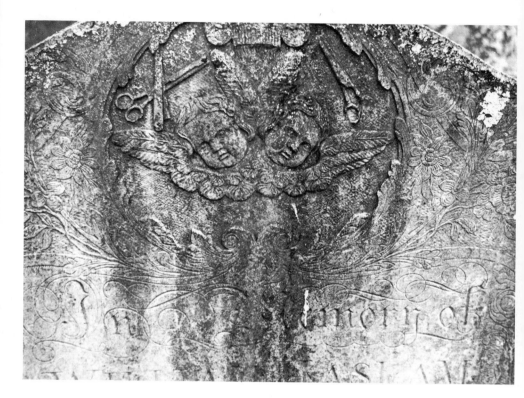

Broadway, Worcestershire: an eighteenth-century barber's gravestone.

righthand side of the illustration of a barber's gravestone? Perhaps you can tell what other tools are shown? Another illustration is of a monument to an artist in the Yorkshire fishing town of Whitby, and the headstone shows his equipment, including easel, palette and mahlstick. It is doubtful if an artist could earn a living in Whitby today, although some do in Cornish seaside towns. It would be interesting to know how this one earned his living in the mid-nineteenth century. What sort of clothes would he have worn, and what was his mahlstick for? You could write a description of a day in the life of an artist working in your town a century ago and illustrate it with drawings such as he might have made of the local scene.

Country life
Until about two centuries ago the majority of people in England and Wales lived and worked in the country. Village churchyards

An artist's gravestone, from the mid-nineteenth century, at Whitby, Yorkshire.

still have many memorials to shepherds, gamekeepers, black-smiths, millers and so on, but few to labourers because their relatives could not afford a stone. As industries developed and more machines were invented, the towns grew larger. Country people moved into the town in search of work. Some country towns became large industrial cities in which you can still some-times find the graves of country craftsmen in the older burial grounds. Other occupations which we now think of as con-nected with industry were once found in the country.

Industry

A small Suffolk village churchyard has the grave of an 'engineer' who died in 1877. How do you think he earned his living? With the rapid growth of industry through the last century living conditions changed, and times were often very hard for working people. Many of you who are now reading this book in school would probably have been out at work by now if you had lived in the early part of the last century and you might have had to do some very unpleasant jobs.

On 6 April 1819 four youths were being lowered down a pit shaft at Little Dean, in the Forest of Dean, when the chain broke and they fell to the bottom. Their tombstone not only gives their names and ages (the youngest was twelve) but also records the whole affair, including details of the funeral service. A far worse accident in a Yorkshire mine in 1838 killed twenty-six miners. The eldest was seventeen and the youngest seven, and there were nearly as many girls as boys. It was incidents such as this which brought the use of child labour to the notice of the public and so helped in the passing of laws forbidding child labour.

The monuments (often paid for by the pit owners) usually have texts and warnings about the power of the Almighty to call forth sudden doom but the majority of people were still able to forget the children working long hours in the mines and mills. Can you imagine what life would have been like for someone of your age a hundred and fifty years ago, and how would you have liked being a pit boy or mill girl in those days?

The monument to the child miners stands in the churchyard at Silkstone, near Barnsley, where there are still many pits. On the other side of the Pennines, at Saddleworth, a monument indicates that not all workpeople were badly treated. It is to a mill owner, and his employees helped to pay for it. Another monument at Saddleworth shows in carved panels all the processes which went into the treatment of wool from the sheep in the fields to the finished product. You can see some of these in the illustration on page 55 and they give a very clear picture of some of the machinery used and the dress which people wore (each workman has a hat). If there are old industries in your area see if you can discover anything about them from monuments in local burial grounds.

Transport

Not all monuments show ancient trades. A pilot's grave at Faringdon, Berkshire, shows a jet aircraft. Travel has always had its dangers and very many monuments give clues as to what

these were and what it must have been like to travel in times
past. Before the building of the canals at the end of the eighteenth century, and the railways in the nineteenth it was very
difficult to travel around the country. Have you noticed how many
family names in old graveyards occur over and over again,
showing that people lived in the same place for many generations? If you make a list of names which occur before 1850 and
compare them with those after 1900 you will find out about this.
When the railways were built and travel became easier for those
who could afford it, the more adventurous moved away from
home in search of their fortune (this is one of the commonest
themes of Victorian stories) and the names in the churchyard
became more varied. During the last century it was still considered worth recording if a man died away from his birthplace
and it was usual to erect a gravestone in his 'home' parish, even
if he died abroad. Even if he had only moved from one village
to the next the fact was sometimes mentioned on his tombstone.
The railways made travel easier but they also had their dangers
both when they were being built and when they were running.
Great engineering works such as tunnels or viaducts often
caused some fatal accidents. In the tiny, remote churchyard at
Chapel le Dale in Yorkshire there are the graves of more than a

*A Victorian woollen
mill on a monument
at Saddleworth,
Yorkshire.*

hundred men who were killed whilst building the Settle to Carlisle Railway. In the churchyard at Otley, also in Yorkshire, a monument in the form of a miniature tunnel was built by the railway company to commemorate the men killed during work on Bramhope Tunnel on the old North Eastern Railway between Leeds and Harrogate. Once the lines were open the dangers were by no means over and crashes and explosions were all too common. A famous monument at Bromsgrove, Worcestershire, commemorates two railwaymen who were killed when a boiler exploded in 1840. The epitaph is based on the working of the engine and starts :

> My engine now is cold and still,
> No water does my boiler fill . . .

Railway gravestones at Bromsgrove, Worcestershire.

The two engines which you can see in the illustrations are correct in every detail. Someone has tried to correct the one on

SACRED
TO THE MEMORY OF THOMAS SCAIFE,
late an Engineer on the Birmingham and Gloucester Railway,
who lost his life at Bromsgrove Station, by the Explosion of
an Engine Boiler on Tuesday the 10 of November 1840.

He was 28 Years of Age, highly esteemed by his fellow workmen
or his many amiable qualities, and his Death will be long lamente
by all those who had the pleasure of his acquaintance.

The following lines were composed by an unknown Friend
as a Memento of the worthiness of the Deceased.

My *engine* now is cold and still. My *flanges* all refuse to guide.
No water does my *boiler* fill. My *clacks*, also, though once so strong,
My *coke* affords its flame no more. Refuse to aid the busy throng.
ty days of usefulness are o'er, No more I feel each urging breath.
My *wheels* deny their noted speed. My *steam* is now condens'd in death.
No more my guiding hands they heed. Life's *railway's* o'er, each *station's* past.
My *whistle* too, has lost its tone. In death I'm stopp'd and rest at last.
Its shrill and thrilling sounds are gone, Farewell dear friends and cease to weep,
My *valves* are now thrown open wide. In Christ I'm SAFE, in Him I sleep.

THIS STONE WAS ERECTED AT THE JOINT EXPENCE
OF HIS FELLOW WORKMEN 1842.

PRATT, Eng.

SACRED
TO THE MEMORY OF
JOSEPH RUTHERFORD,
LATE ENGINEER TO THE BIRMINGHAM AND GLOUCESTER
RAILWAY COMPANY
who Died Nov 11 1840 Aged 32 Years

Oh! Reader stay, and cast an eye,
Upon this Grave wherein I lie.
For cruel Death has challenged me.
And soon alas, will call on thee :
Repent in time, make no delay,
For Christ will call you all away.

My time was spent like day in sun.
Beyond all cure my glass is ru

STONE WAS ERECTED BY HIS AFFECTIONATE

the right by painting in a steam dome, but drawings in the Science Museum show that the original stone-carver was right to leave it out. A train enthusiast could make an accurate model and drawings from this memorial.

Ships

Seaside graveyards have many memorials to men who died at sea, and they often record the event in detail. Many show sailing ships and a history of sailing ships could be compiled from them. In a churchyard in a field at Llanfihangel-din-Salwy on the island of Anglesey a whole fleet of boats has been scratched into the slate tombstones by someone who must have spent hours watching the ships pass. These make good rubbings, but more often ships are carved in low relief and are best copied by drawing. Some are clear enough to provide details for your own models. Not all ships are found near the sea, as seafaring men

Llanfihangel-din-Salwy, Anglesey.

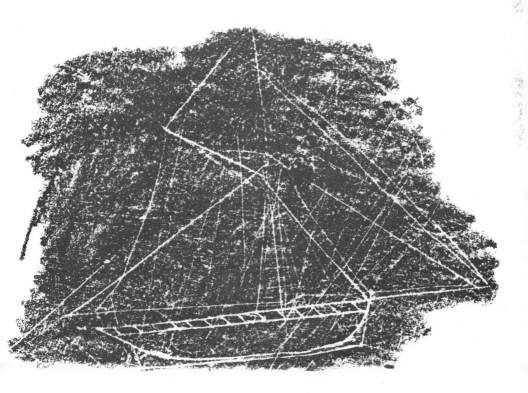

Newnham-on-Severn, Gloucestershire: an accurate record of a boating accident in 1848.

Great Yarmouth, Norfolk: 1845, the bridge collapses, a boatman clings to the bank and the eye of God looks down on the scene.

often came from inland families. At Lamplugh in the Lake Dis-
trict, for example, a memorial to a captain who was drowned off
Jamaica in 1817 has a realistic carving of a ship on a rough sea.
Why would his ship have been in the West Indies?

Accidents happen on inland waterways as well as on the seas.
In 1848 two young men were drowned after a collision in the
River Severn. The epitaph tells the story and the carving, as you
can see, shows the boats involved and the two boys in the water.
One of the ships is a paddle-steamer with some barrels on deck.
What do you think it might have been carrying, and to or from
which ports? The paddle-steamer also has a mast and sails.
New inventions always had their dangers. A suspension bridge
collapsed in Yarmouth in 1845, killing a nine-year-old boy.
From the illustration of the carving on his tombstone you can see
the collapsed bridge, and the rescue boats in the water beneath.
From it you could easily reconstruct the bridge, with its masonry
piers, decorative railings and suspension towers. Above the
bridge the eye of God looks down on the scene of the tragedy.
Find out when the first suspension bridge was built, and look for
any monuments which show that inventions were not always as
safe as they should have been.

All kinds of professions, trades and skills (including that of
schoolboy) are shown or described on memorials. You can trace
the history of some towns or villages by noting the changes in
occupations recorded, whilst in other places they have remained
very much the same for centuries. Nowadays it is very unusual
for a trade or profession to be mentioned on a stone and it would
be interesting to find out why this is. How would you show such
modern occupations as scientist or computer operator; astro-
naut or pop singer?

8   Living things

Plant and animal life in churchyards

Many people think of graveyards as 'dead' places and yet many of them are the best places to go to find all sorts of living things. This is so whether you live in the town or in the country. In the middle of the town an old graveyard may be the only place for miles where plants are allowed to grow without being tidied into gardens, where many birds can find nesting places and where insects can live undisturbed. In the country, when more and more farmers are using chemicals to destroy weeds and insects the local churchyard can become just as much of a wild-life sanctuary as those in towns.

Old prints often show country churchyards with sheep grazing among the tombstones. The grasses which grew between the stones were too good to waste, and the vicar was allowed to sell the grazing to a local farmer. By doing so he added to his own income, helped the farmer and solved the problem of keeping the churchyard tidy. Nowadays it is very unusual to find sheep in a churchyard. Can you think why this is? The photograph of sheep in the churchyard at Linton-in-Craven was taken very recently and the scene cannot have changed much for a century. You may be able to find one thing which has been added. Notice how the grass is short enough for you to be able to walk around without difficulty and yet there are still plenty of wild flowers.

Some people like to see the churchyard looking like a lawn, with the grass cut short and most of the monuments cleared away. When this is done most of the wild life disappears and the grave-yard is much less interesting. It looks just like any other garden. The photographs show what a churchyard can look like when the grasses and wild plants are allowed to grow. Look at the picture of the churchyard at Cwmyoy in Monmouthshire. Do you think that this looks untidy? Some people would prefer it if the grass were cut short and the old stones made into a wall round

Sheep in the churchyard at Linton-in-Craven, Yorkshire.

Cwmyoy, Monmouthshire: the abundant plant life of a churchyard. How many different kinds of plants, insects and animals would you expect to find there?

Family graves together at St Just in Roseland, Cornwall.

the edge. Even in this country district you can see that there are far more plants in the churchyard than in the fields beyond. The path is kept clear from growth so that you can walk to the church door without difficulty and yet the graveyard itself is like a miniature jungle. The stones are like strange animals amid the undergrowth and some of them are nearly hidden. The photograph of St Just in Roseland, Cornwall shows a churchyard which is even more like a jungle with its sub-tropical trees. If you look at these pictures you can imagine all kinds of birds, insects and small animals hiding among the plants.

One of the best places to find insect life is on old stones covered by ivy. If you pulled the ivy away from the stones in the pictures what do you think you would find? Often you will find stinging nettles in churchyards. Obviously gardeners do not like nettles

Plants overgrowing old stones at Dumbleton, Gloucestershire. How much plant life is there and how much would be pulled up as weeds in a garden?

and they soon destroy them, but the caterpillars of some of our most beautiful butterflies feed on nettles. Without the nettles there would be no more of these butterflies. Is this a good enough reason for letting a few nettles survive in the churchyard?

Lichens

The tombstone at Dumbleton has even more plants growing on or around it. On the stone itself you can see patches of dark and light which are made by plants called lichens. They show up much more on the photograph taken at Portland. Lichens are very strange plants. They grow extremely slowly and they can live in extremes of heat and cold as well as for a long time without water. What they do not like is pollution of the atmosphere, and

Multi-coloured lichens on a white Portland stone monument on the Isle of Portland, Dorset.

for this reason you will not find many in industrial areas. They cannot even live in those parts of the country where the prevailing winds blow across from the polluted areas. But Portland sticks out into the English Channel and the sea air is very clean, so the lichens thrive there. Portland stone is very white and so the many colours of the lichens are particularly noticeable there. The colours of lichens are very varied and they range from bright orange to pale grey. The plants themselves are so inconspicuous that they often pass unnoticed and people think that it is the stones on which they grow which are coloured. Have a closer look at the lichens, if there are any, in your local graveyard. They grow on trees as well as on stones. Draw their various shapes and, if you have a microscope, see what they are like when magnified. They are much more interesting than they seem to be at first glance.

Plants and insects

A good way to discover the amount of wild life in a graveyard is to mark off several areas of about a square metre each, in different parts, and to make a list of all the wild living things you can find in each. You might even hold a competition to see who can find the most. You will be surprised not only by the number of different things but also by the way in which different parts of the same graveyard can produce different collections. If your local churchyard has been cleared and mown you may have to look elsewhere for a great variety of things but even grass harbours many insects, and there are many varieties of grass.

If you can find a way of marking each area that you investigate, perhaps by drawing a detailed plan, you can return to them at different times of the year and discover how they change. In summer the plants are growing and multi-coloured and other forms of life use them for food and shelter. In the winter the dead plants often remain although the colours may not be as varied as the shapes are. The dried seed-heads of dead plants and even dead grasses can be very beautiful. You can collect some and stick them on to sheets of coloured paper. Others can be arranged in jars or vases.

Hunt among the plants and you may find all sorts of things. Grubs and caterpillars need the plants for food. Spiders spin their webs between them. Chrysalids are buried just beneath the ground or hidden in the curl of leaves. In the daytime moths hide under leaves, or on the bark of trees. There is so much to find that you will not be able to write it all down, and everything is changing all the time.

Change and growth

As each season's growth dies off and new plants grow each year the level of the ground gradually changes. Have you noticed how many inscriptions seem to be half buried? Sometimes old stones, particularly ledger stones, get buried and plants cover them over. You can often discover old stones by prodding the surface of the ground with a pointed stick. At Saddleworth in Yorkshire many of the old gravestones are ledgers, and the moorland grasses have completely covered some of them. You can tell where they are when you walk across them, for the ground is much softer around them. When you have found one you can peel the grass off like a mat, as you can see in the photograph. This 'mat' consists entirely of the roots of grasses and small plants which seem to thrive on the moisture which collects on the stone. The roots are so fine, and they grow so close together that every mark on the surface of the stone shows in reverse on the mat. Even a slight crack in the stone is filled with grass roots and shows quite clearly.

A flat stone completely covered by grass at Saddleworth, Yorkshire. The grass roots take a perfect impression from the stone.

Trees

Trees have always been associated with burial grounds and sacred places. The ancient Greeks had their 'sacred groves' and yew trees marked sacred places in this country even before the coming of Christianity. Evergreens have often been used by

Christians as a symbol of eternal life and so they are very common in old graveyards. Sometimes small bushes of holly, or other evergreens, were planted on graves and many of these have now become large trees. Many of the yews in graveyards are hundreds of years old and although their foliage is poisonous they shelter many kinds of birds. There are few churchyards which have no trees and every tree attracts other forms of life. In fact, a tree is more like a wild-life city than a single plant.

If you look long enough, and carefully enough, you may discover an owl's sleeping place from the pellets of discarded beetles' wings or mice bones which collect around it. You may see a snake basking in the sunlight on a path, if it does not see you first and disappear. It is quite likely that you may discover a butterfly or moth, spider or beetle, which has not been noticed before in your district. If you are patient you will find that the discoveries which you can make are endless. Local natural history societies can often give you help and advice and they would almost certainly be interested to hear about any discoveries which you make. A book of churchyard life, perhaps kept like a diary over a year, would be very interesting, particularly if it were illustrated with drawings, photographs, pressed plants and prints from leaves.

Sources of information

The best sources of information are the graveyards themselves. Apart from the obvious churchyards and cemeteries it is worth looking for nonconformist burial grounds, Quaker graveyards (often unmarked and only to be traced from old maps) and closed graveyards. Closed churchyards are often the responsibility of the local authority.

Recent books
Very few books have been written about churchyards or the design of gravestones. The two which will be found most useful are :
Of Graves and Epitaphs by Kenneth Lindley (Hutchinson).
English Churchyard Memorials by Frederick Burgess (Lutterworth).
The Church Information Office publishes a useful booklet called *The Churchyards' Handbook* which is intended as a guide for those responsible for the care of churchyards.

Old books
Books of epitaphs have always been popular and they can often be bought quite cheaply in second-hand bookshops. Among the most interesting (and popular) are :
Johnson's Epitaphs (with an essay by Dr Johnson) (1806).
Chronicles of the Tombs by T. J. Pettigrew (1857).
Epitaphs Quaint, Curious & Elegant by H. J. Loaring.
Curious Epitaphs by William Andrews (1899).
Faithful Servants by Arthur J. Munby, published in 1891, is an excellent example of how graveyards can be used as sources of social history.
Another book entitled *A Collection of Curious and Interesting Epitaphs, copied from the existing monuments of Distinguished and Noted Characters in The Cemeteries and Churchyards of*

Saint Pancras, Middlesex, by Frederick Teague Cansick gives a
lively cross-section of Victorian society. It was published in
1872.
W. T. Vincent's *In Search of Gravestones Old and Curious,*
published in 1896, shows what can be done by anyone interested in recording the gravestones of a particular area. It is a
collection of drawings and inscriptions from the churchyards of
Kent, Essex and elsewhere together with interesting personal
comments and consists mainly of records of visits made on foot.
The preface begins 'I am a gravestone rambler and I beg you to
bear me company' and it claims to be the first book devoted to
'common gravestones'. Most books on church monuments
(including Katherine Esdaile's standard work *English Church
Monuments 1510–1840*) ignore the humble tombstones,
although they are mentioned in Lawrence Weaver's *Memorials
and Monuments* (1915) and W. H. Godfrey's *English Mural
Monuments and Tombstones* (1916). On churchyard lore, customs and superstitions the most interesting work was published
in 1858. It is called *God's Acre, or Historical Notices relating to
Churchyards*, and written by Mrs Stone.

Magazines
The most useful journal on the subject is *Commemorative Art,*
the stonemason's trade magazine. Both *Country Life* and the
Architectural Review publish articles on churchyards and
monuments.

Background
For background material both the poets and painters of the
eighteenth and nineteenth centuries provide plenty of sources.
Apart from the well-known examples such as Arthur Hughes's
painting 'Home from the Sea' (Ashmolean Museum) or Gray's
'Elegy in a Country Churchyard' there are numerous delightful
prints, illustrations and watercolours by minor artists, and poems
by country clergymen, which give the atmosphere of the churchyard.
Perhaps the best modern poem on the subject is 'Churchyards'
by Sir John Betjeman, contained in the collection *Poems in the*

Porch. John Piper, who illustrated these, has done many paintings of English churchyards and the Shell Guides which he edits are one of the few series of county guide books ever to mention gravestones.

Methods

Various books on print making explain techniques for making prints from stone and other surfaces. The most useful is that by Michael Rothenstein, *Frontiers of Printmaking,* published by Studio Vista. The best book on rubbings (although devoted to brass rubbings, not rubbings from tombstones) is Henry Trivick's *The Craft and Design of Monumental Brasses* published by John Baker. For techniques of observing and recording generally, the Townlook series, edited by Gordon Boon and published by Pergamon, will be found most useful. *Chapels and Meeting Houses* by Kenneth Lindley deals with nonconformist burial grounds.

It is always interesting to talk to somebody who knows a lot about a subject you are studying, and your local vicar, minister or cemeteries superintendent could be helpful. A visit to a stonemason's yard can be very rewarding. Many Quaker Meetings have old books which contain advice to Quakers about avoiding vanity in inscriptions and monuments and the library of Friends House, Euston Road, London has a good collection of these.

Acknowledgments

The author and publishers would like to thank Sir John Betjeman and John Murray (Publishers) Ltd for permission to reproduce an extract from 'Churchyards', from *Collected Poems*.